By: EricSkaggs.com , TheYouTubeGuy.com ,
IInventedYouTube.com

Here is the $1 million deal:

I will give you $1,000,000 if you help me get the $16.5 million
ChadHurley.com promised me for the YouTube idea I gave
him. I must actually get the the 1% or $16.5 million from the
YouTube idea I gave Chad Hurley.to give you the $1 million
reward, but I am confident we can do this.

To read the first chapter of this book for free, buy this book
and/or share this book with your friends and collect your $1
million reward, go to these websites and contribute ideas:

http://www.IInventedYouTube.com

http://www.TheYouTubeGuy.com

http://www.WhoInventedYouTube.com

To read the first chapter of this book for free, buy this book
and/or share this book with your friends, go to these websites:

http://www.YouScrewd.com

http://www.TheRealYouTubeStory.com

http://www.RealYouTubeStory.com

http://www.TheYouTubeStory.com

To get in touch with Eric Skaggs, go to EricSkaggs.com

To visit Eric Skaggs's new website, go to BuckGet.com

To get in touch with Chad Hurley, go to ChadHurley.com

YouTube : TheREALYouTubeStory.com

The true story of how EricSkaggs.com invented YouTube and gave ChadHurley.com the YouTube.com idea from domain name to exit strategy in exchange for a promise of 1% or $16.5 million.

Table of contents :

Chapter 1: IInventedYouTube.com

I was finishing up some work on my website at the Eberly College of Business computer lab at Indiana University of Pennsylvania in 1999 at 8pm. I was the last person to leave the lab, as usual. As I closed the door behind me, I saw a tall guy wearing a baseball cap with a bag slung over his shoulder coming in the side door of the building. There was nothing else open in the building but the computer lab and he looked like he was in a hurry to get there.

I said to him"I guess you're here to use the computer lab. It closes at 8pm. It's exactly 8 now". He looked disappointed and tried to convince me to let him in. I think he thought I ran the computer lab.

I said to him"I think the computer lab in the computer science building is open till 9 but you might not make it there on time because it's all the way on the other side of campus. I come here all the time to work on my website because this is the best computer lab on campus and I used to live across the street at McGregor hall so I can park over there".

He suddenly got very interested.

"You have a website?"he asked."What kind of website? I want to start a website but I can't think of a website to start. Can you give me a good idea for a website?"

I said "My website is called GoGetItNow.com. It's an internet portal that combines the free search capabilities of Yahoo, the free web pages of Geocities and the free email of Hotmail into one interface. It gets 10 million page views a day, makes $5000 a month and it's doubling every couple of months."

Now He was really excited. We introduced ourselves to each other. He told me his name was Chad and he was a graphic arts major on a track scholarship and he was graduating that semester. We talked as we walked to the front doors of the building.

Chad persisted "I have been learning html on my own in my spare time. If you could give me a great idea for a website, I am sure I could make it work".

We walked out the doors of Eberly and toward a yellow Jeep. "Is that your Jeep?" I said.

He halfheartedly said "Yes", but I found out later it wasn't his. He must've borrowed it.

"I love it" I said. "My step dad has one just like it but his is black. It might look better if it was black, but it is kinda cool and different. I am driving that little red 3 series BMW over there, but I would much rather drive an American car. That Beamer makes me feel like a pretentious yuppie. I miss my Camaro I traded for it. I love cars, but I can't get into Nascar. Isn't it strange how there is no formula one racing team in America? When you get rich from this idea I give you, you should start a formula one racing team in America."

He said "That's a great idea. I will. Now what's your idea?".

Chad did try to start a formula one race team in the US like I told him to do, but he failed, as he failed with everything else in his life after the YouTube idea I gave him.

I said "I'll give you the idea, but first, you have to promise me three things. When you are rich from this idea I give you, you have to let me hang out on your private island, ride around on your yacht, and you have to give me 1% of the company."

He said impatiently "Okay."

I repeated "You promise to give me 1% of the company?"

He reiterated "Yes. I promise. Now what's the idea?"

I said "Now pay attention. This is the most important idea anyone will ever give you. Just do exactly what I say and you will be successful."

Chad eagerly said "I will".

I said "Okay. In the future, television and computers with internet will become one. People will start using their cellphones to make videos like they are camcorders".

Chad looked confused, and for good reason. At that time, they were just coming out with camera phones, and there were no video phones. There was a rumor of a cellphone that could take 5 second video clips of poor quality, but not many people knew about it except for those that kept up with such things like myself. And television and internet were considered two very different things back then. Despite his skepticism, I convinced him it would happen and continued.

"When they take these videos, they are going to want to share them with friends, family and the world. I said "It will be like everybody has their own television channel on on the internet."

YouTube.com allows users to share their videos and create their own "channels" as I said to Chad.

They will need a website to do that. It will be called something funny like Yahoo. What's a funny thing to call a tv? I got it. BoobTube.com." We laughed for a while and talked about how it had the word "Boob" in it and sounded like an adult website.

I said "Take the word "Boob" out and put in another word. The website is about people sharing videos so put a pronoun in there. If you conjugate a verb, the pronouns are I, you, he, she, it, we, you, they, and I said "You" twice. YouTube.com. That sounds good. Get YOU tube.com and utube.com."

This was the first time anybody ever said "YouTube.com". I said "YouTube.com" to Chad, the founder of YouTube.com in 1999 and he registered the domain name YouTube.com about 5 years later in 2004.

When Chad went to register the domain names I told him to use about five years later, utube.com was taken by a tubing company so he could only get YouTube.com.

We said "YouTube.com" back and forth to each other a couple of times and agreed that it sounded great.

It is well documented that Chad said he used boobtube, a way to refer to television, that later became YouTube.com. I gave Chad the name YouTube.com and used boobtube as a guide. He just pretended he came up with YouTube.com.

At this point, we were pretty excited about this YouTube.com idea. Chad anxiously awaited the rest of my idea. He was hanging on my every word.

I said "No offense, but you are on an athletic scholarship, not an academic scholarship and you are studying graphic art, not computer science, at a low level state school, not an ivy league school, so the first thing you have to do is find some smart people to help you build the website and for credibility. I would help you and work with you, but I am busy with GoGetItNow. You will have to get a job in the dot com industry. Do you have a portfolio of graphic designs you can send to dot com companies to show them that you can design logos and graphics for them?"

He said "Not really".

I said "Get really good at making digital graphics".

Chad promised me he would learn how to make digital graphics.

I said "Go to Giant Eagle (the local grocery store) and grab the latest Wired magazine. There is a great article in there with a list of all the top up and coming website companies. Redesign their logos and send them to the companies. Make them simple and nice."

It is well documented that Chad Hurley found his first job at PayPal in a Wired magazine. He applied to and got a job at PayPal.com where he designed the logo, a very simple logo.

I said "When you get a job for a dot com company, you will need to find the smartest guys in the room to make the website and for credibility. It will probably be a really smart Asian guy and a really smart Indian guy from top level technology oriented universities with advanced computer science degrees."

Chad got Steve Chen and Jawed Karim, the smartest guys in the room and the Asian and Indian guys he worked with at PayPal, to help him with YouTube.

I said "You will need to beg borrow and steal money to get the website going and keep it going. Finding the most bandwidth for the least amount of money will be a top priority too because all those videos will use a lot of bandwidth."

Chad got a lot of cheap bandwidth from a company in the area. YouTube was kicked off the servers when YouTube used almost all of the unlimited bandwidth.

We started talking about ways to raise money and I had another brainstorm.

I said "While you are down at Giant Eagle getting the Wired magazine, grab the new Forbes list of the richest people magazine that just came out and make a list of the top richest dot com guys. Figure out where they go. Go where they go. Get to know them. You will need them to help you fund YouTube. And figure out if any of those rich guys have single daughters around your age. Figure out where they go. Start at the top of the list. Follow her around. Do whatever you have to do to get her pregnant and marry her."

That was such a shocking statement, we had to stop and think about it for a while. It really is the best way to get rich. Get a rich girl pregnant and she will most likely marry you.

Despite it sounding like a joke, we agreed he would have to do it, and it seems like he did. He crashed a birthday party for someone he didn't know where a woman named Kathy Clark was. He went right up to Kathy Clark at the party. They are married with two children. Kathy Clark is the heiress to the Silicon Graphics fortune and her father, Jim Clark, was on the

Forbes list of the riches people. He is also a venture capitalist and I don't see how YouTube.com would've made it through the lean years without the help of Kathy Clark and her billionaire venture capitalist father Jim Clark. Kathy would've been at the top of the list I told Chad to make.

I said "Some videos will get shared with others and they will share them and so on. There will be exponential growth(we didn't call it viral back then because of the negative implications). Everybody will get their 15 minutes of fame and some people will become stars."

YouTube.com did get big fast and grew exponentially as I predicted. We really started seeing how big something like this would be.

I said "It will take so much money to do something like this. You will be able to make a little bit of money selling ads around the videos and in the videos like commercials, but you won't make real money until you sell YouTube to a company with more money than brains like Yahoo(Google didn't exist yet), and if GoGetItNow is big enough by then, I will buy YouTube."

Chad Hurley did sell YouTube to "A company with more money than brains". That company was called Google.com and he sold YouTube.com to Google.com for approximately $1.65 billion.

I said "It's going to take so much money, you will need to constantly go around to venture capitalists, angel investors, banks, and anyone you can get to listen to you to raise money, but make sure you never give up controlling interest in YouTube. Give up percentages of the company for money, but never so much that you lose control of the company.

Chad was able to retain 20% of the company, which was controlling interest. Steve Chen kept 19% and Jawed Karim got a small percentage since he left the company before it was sold. Chad was able to get approximately $330 million for the YouTube.com idea I gave him.

I continued "When you ask for money for YouTube, you are going to have to tell them it's your idea or you won't have any credibility. They aren't going to give you any money if you tell them I gave you the idea. You are going to need a plausible back story. Make up a story about how you and some friends were at a party taking videos with your camcorders and maybe the technology will be available to take videos with your phones by then, and you wanted to share them with each other and couldn't so you created a website to share videos with each other called YouTube."

Chad still insists he came up with the YouTube idea when he, Steve and Jawed were at a party taking videos with their camcorders and phones and couldn't share them with each other so they created YouTube.com. That is the exact story I told Chad to use. Steve Chen and Jawed Karim both said later that Chad lied about the story he told. There was never any party where they were taking videos. Steve and Jawed say Chad made up the story. The actual story of how YouTube.com started is I gave Chad Hurley the entire idea from domain name to exit strategy and everything in between. It is this story.

By now, it was after 9pm and all the computer labs were closed on campus.

After the excitement of our conversation, I asked him where he hangs out in Indiana. He said he doesn't really go out much. He said they have parties in the cross country house. I asked him when he was leaving IUP and he said he was graduating this semester and was just back to pick up the last of his things. He didn't want to hang out with me. He wanted to go to Giant Eagle and get started on YouTube.

I reiterated the promise he made to give me 1%, he agreed he would fulfill his promise, and we parted ways.

I never thought much about Chad and the 1 percent he promised me for the YouTube idea I gave him. I just worked really hard on GoGetItNow until two things happened that ended my dream. First, as I was trying to take GoGetItNow public, the .com bubble burst. Smith Barney called me a week before the meeting with them to go public and said they had to reevaluate dot com's and basically, they weren't interested anymore.

Then, my website went down. I called my server administrator, Chris, at Cyberwurx in Atlanta, Georgia, and he said it was on Network Solution's end. I called Network Solutions and after getting bounced around from one person to another, someone said "rogue call center workers" at their India office were cancelling domain names that were popular and renewing them privately. The company that took GoGetItNow is still in existence. It is called ITSSN.com. There was a class action lawsuit, but I don't believe it went anywhere because I don't think anyone knew who stole all the domain names and they couldn't be extradited.

I let my dream die and went back to college using grants and loans from FAFSA. I graduated from Indiana University of Pennsylvania with a degree in business with an emphasis in finance and computer science in 2002. I went on to become a financial advisor for a wall street firm, Merrill Lynch, but quickly realized that being a stockbroker was basically about helping rich people get richer. I wanted to help everyone including those that needed the most help. I became a Social Worker and quickly realized you couldn't really help people because of all the bureaucracy. It was right around that time that I realized the guy I met and gave the YouTube idea to, Chad Hurley, did very well with my YouTube idea, so I started my own website to help people without the ugliness of wall street or the bureaucracy of social services. That website is called BuckGet.com .

When I heard about YouTube in about 2005 or 2006, I thought "What a coincidence. I gave some guy named Chad an idea for a video sharing website called YouTube.com back at IUP in 1999", but I never could've dreamed it was the same guy.

In about 2011, my ex girlfriend Coryn said something about YouTube and I said to her "I gave some guy named Chad an idea for a video sharing website I called YouTube back at IUP in 1999. He promised me one percent of the company. And now this YouTube thing is huge. What a coincidence right?"

She said, "Eric. You know the guy that started YouTube went to IUP don't you?"

I said, "No. I didn't know that. Wouldn't it be funny if his name was Chad?"

I went over to the computer and googled something like "Chad IUP YouTube".

I couldn't believe it! It was him! Chad Hurley! I never knew his last name until that moment. He looked just like he did in 1999. He had long hair and was relatively tall and decent looking. I continued my googleing and reading. He went to IUP on a track scholarship and was a graphic design major. He got a Wired magazine, sent a logo redesign to PayPal and got a job there. He partnered up with the smartest guys in the room. They were an Asian guy named Steve Chen and an Indian guy named Jawed Karim. He crashed a birthday party to meet and marry Kathy Clark, the heiress to Jim Clark's Silicon Graphics fortune. He registered the domain name YouTube.com as a video sharing website in 2004 and launched YouTube on valentine's day 2005. YouTube got huge quickly as I predicted. He sold the YouTube idea I gave him in 2007 to Google, the "company with more money than brains" for $1.65 billion! He did everything I told him to do. He even tried to start a formula one race team.

He promised me and owes me one percent of YouTube and he sold YouTube for $1.65 billion! Chad Hurley owes me $16.5 million!

I tried to contact Chad. I connected with him on Twitter and I was blocked. I tried to friend him on Facebook. I was blocked again. I found his phone number and talked to his housekeeper, I think her name was Anne, for about a half an hour. She was very nice and said Chad would definitely want to talk to me about my new ideas. I emailed Chad at all his email addresses. I applied for jobs at Google, YouTube, Avos, Delicious and all the companies Chad was involved with. I never got a response.

I emailed Roelof Botha, one of the first venture capitalists to back YouTube.com. I don't think he believed me when I emailed the story of my involvement with YouTube. He thanked me for the "color" in the email I sent him. I don't think he believed me or wanted to believe me.

Chad never contacted me in any way. I searched the internet to see if there was any mention of me and YouTube. I found an old newspaper clipping that said YouTube was a play on words from BoobTube. That's how I came up with the name. I found the story I told Chad to tell people about how he and some friends were taking videos at a party and couldn't share them with each other so he created a website with Steve Chen and Jawed Karim called YouTube. There was no mention of me and why would there be? I told Chad he would have to lie and he did.

My searching led me to a guy named Herb that said he invented YouTube and we messaged each other for a while on YouTube. I found out Herb had an attorney in Pittsburgh. The attorney met with me and said he couldn't represent me because they already represented Herb. I said "Why would you represent somebody who lied and not me when I am telling the truth?" He indicated it was simply a conflict of interests, but I should continue to try to reach Chad. I was never able to reach him.

It was suggested that I document my story or even write a book by some filmmakers so that is what I am doing.

The rest of this book is about what Chad did after our conversation outside the Eberly College of Business computer lab at Indiana University of Pennsylvania.

My hope is that Chad will fulfill his promise and give me the 1% or approximately $16.5 million he promised me. If he does fulfill his promise, we can work together on the other projects I have ideas for and I may even take the real story, this story, off the internet to protect Chad's reputation. If Chad doesn't want to work with me, maybe this would make a nice documentary in the style of "Social Network" and maybe I will get what was promised to me anyways.

Since I was laid off and trying to get in touch with Chad Hurley about YouTube and the one percent he promised me, I decided to start a new website called BuckGet.com dedicated to helping people find ways to earn a living online. It started doing very well very fast. BuckGet.com had about 717,000 members in its first year. While I worked on BuckGet.com, I called around to see if I could get a lawyer to help me get in touch with Chad since I had no luck on my own. A really great intellectual property attorney named Louis Kroeck said he would help me get an answer as to whether or not Chad was going to fulfill his promise and give me $16.5 million. We sent a letter to Chad asking him to speak with us. We got a threatening letter from a high priced law firm that represented Chad known as Wilson Sonsini Goodrich and Rosati.

The big question was finally answered. Not only did Chad not want to resolve this amicably, he wanted to throw insults and threats at me. He started tweeting things about how he thought I need to "get help" and called me crazy. His attorneys asked me to cease and desist. That just made me want to get the story out to everyone.

I registered the domain names IInventedYouTube.com , TheYouTubeGuy.com and WhoInventedYouTube.com and put the story on those domain names.

I put out a reward of $165,000 to anyone that could help me get the $16.5 million Chad Hurley owes me. I updated the reward to $1,000,000 recently!

I continued working on a book I call "YouScrewed: The REAL YouTube Story".

I got the custom license plate for Pennsylvania that says YouTube and put WWW.THE YOUTUBE GUY.COM on the front of my car and the custom license plate for Pennsylvania that says BUCKGET and put WWW.BUCKGET.COM on the back of my car.

I wear t shirts that say BuckGet on them almost every day.

Most people think Chad Hurley started YouTube in 2005 and sold it in 2007 for $1.65 billion but I know Chad started working on YouTube when I gave him the idea in 1999 and fulfilled his contract with Google in 2010, so I am giving myself the same 11 years to work on BuckGet.com as Chad spent on YouTube.com.

BuckGet.com is doing very well, but I get little to no support from the Pittsburgh technology community mostly because most people don't take the time to really understand the YouTube Story and automatically assume I am lying.

I have truth, time and the first amendment on my side as I diligently work on BuckGet.com and IInventedYouTube.com .

I am planning a trip to Silicon Valley to see if I can make it there with BuckGet.com and maybe even to do a little investigative reporting on Chad Hurley. It would be irresponsible of me to write a book on Chad Hurley and YouTube without doing some hands on research.

Stay tuned for updates and if you can help me and had the patience to read this, call me at (724)840-2654.

Thank you,

www.EricSkaggs.com

www.TheYouTubeGuy.com

www.WhoInventedYouTube.com

www.IInventedYouTube.com

Founder of www.BuckGet.com

Chapter 2: EricSkaggs.com

Here comes the fun part. I get to talk about myself. I'm being sarcastic, but they don't have punctuation to express sarcasm...do they? People have told me that this is the best part because I tell it all just like it is and my life is pretty screwed up. Here we gooooo...

I, EricSkaggs.com , was born on September 13th, 1973 in Morgantown, West Virginia. So I am already disadvantaged. Branded for life as a backwoods mountain redneck hillbilly.

My father, CraigSkaggs.com, had just received a master's degree in public relations from West Virginia University and my mother, RosemarySkaggs.com , had just received a bachelor's degree in nursing from West Virginia University. The name on my birth certificate said "Grayson Eric Skaggs" , although I didn't find out my real first name was Grayson until I got my driver's license when I was 16. That created a real identity crisis, but since no one ever called me Grayson, I consider my name to be Eric.

I know why my name is Grayson. That was my grandfather on my dad's sides name and my dad told me it was some sick president's doctors name and he really ran the country for a while and my great grandparents thought very highly of Doctor Grayson. When I was 10, I asked my mom why she and my dad named me Eric and she told me it was because my dad had red pubic hair and my mom's pet name for his penis was Eric The Red, so I was named after my dad's penis! I found that quite disturbing and hilarious.

My mom always had a sibling rivalry with her only sibling, my uncle Grant Myers II, so when She found out Grant was marrying his wife, Denise, my mom asked my dad to marry her and he did. When my mom found out my uncle Grant and aunt Denise were having their first child, my cousin Susan, my mom asked my dad if they could have a child and they did...me. So I was the result of a sibling rivalry and named after a penis. Not a good start to life. To make things worse, when Grant and Denise found out they were having another child, my cousin Grant III, my mom asked my dad if they could have another child and my dad said all he ever wanted was a son and he had that. He was done. So my mom left my dad with the excuse that he drank and smoked too much to pursue a man that claimed to be a wealthy DuPont descendent named Ed Weisbrod.

When I was about two years old, my mom packed me and some luggage up in the station wagon with the wood grained sides and moved to Wilmington, Delaware. She became a nurse for Blue Cross and Blue Shield, and they paid for her to get her Masters degree in hospital administration at Temple University.

My dad moved to Wilmington, Delaware soon after to be closer to me and to climb the corporate ladder at DuPont, where he became a very successful public relations executive. His claim to fame is he is the guy that saved the planet by helping to ban Chloro Flouro Carbons(CFC's) that were eating a hole in the ozone layer. He once showed me a golden statue of a guy holding up a globe in the lobby of the DuPont building that he earned for his efforts.

My dad soon remarried a woman named Jackie who had a son from a previous marriage named Jay. My dad says he was trying to fill the void in his life my mom left when she left him for Ed Weisbrod.

I remember alot of horseback riding and balloon riding when I was younger from Ed Weisbrod's wealthy family. I even had a pony named Sonny, but Ed never wanted to marry my mother because she had a kid, me. And Ed wasn't as wealthy as he claimed to be. My dad actually ended up being wealthier than Ed.

Eventually, my mom got sick of kicking people out of the hospital that didn't have health insurance, the primary job of a hospital administrator, and my uncle Grant suggested she do like he did and start a State Farm Insurance agency, so when I was 6, my mom quit her job and we moved to the Pittsburgh area(Scottdale, Connellsville and Mount Pleasant area) so my mom could, once again, beat my uncle Grant. She did do much better than uncle grant financially, but she struggles to this day with failed relationships and uncle Grant is still married to Denise, so who really "won"?

I went to a small Catholic school in Scottdale, Pennsylvania called Saint John's from the ages of 5 to 12 because even though I did well enough academically to get into first grade in the public school system, I was too young and my mom wanted me to go to first grade early so she could work on her business and to help me excel academically.

I was a nerd and a runt, but none of the 12 people in my class knew I was a year younger than them. They picked on me for getting straight A's and being smaller than them.

Since my mom was so busy building her successful State Farm Insurance agency, I got to spend a lot of time with my grandparents that lived in the adjoining town of Connellsville. My grandfather, Grant Senior, ended up being more of a father to me than a grandfather. I rarely saw my father, who was now living in the Philadelphia area where he spent almost all of his working live working his way up the corporate ladder at DuPont and building what looked like a very nice new family with his new wife and son Jackie and Jay.

I went back and forth from the Pittsburgh area to the Philadelphia area when I was younger, but I consider myself a Pittsburgher.

In 8th grade, my teacher, Mrs. Kovalchick, gave me the first failing grade I ever got in my life and I flipped out. It was a test about conjugating verbs. That's kind of ironic since I used my ability to conjugate verbs to come up with the YouTube.com domain name. I insisted on switching schools, and my mom let me.

For most of the 8th grade, I got to go to the same school my mom went to, Connellsville East. We lived in the woods at the time and I spent alot of time drawing, painting, sculpting, riding my go cart, three wheeler and quad dirt bikes, and, until the age of 8, reading.

When I was in second grade, my teacher...I can't remember her name(Maple? Plum?...I think it sounded edible), had a reading competition, so I read hundreds of books. I read books at lunch, between classes, during classes, after school, until I went to sleep, and from the time I woke up in the morning to the time I got to school. I won the reading contest and the teacher had me come to the front of the class to accept the secret reward for all of my hard work. She opened up her desk, rummaged around and pulled something rubber off of the end of a pencil. It was a pencil eraser protector. Everybody laughed at me. The teacher told me the real reward was reading all of those books.

I vowed to never read a book I didn't have to read ever again. I was reading at a college level in first grade, and I probably read at a college level today.

As a matter of a fact, in first grade, I got in trouble for reading "The Yearling" . My teacher thought I stole her book. How could a 6 or 7 year old kid be reading "The Yearling"? She stopped yelling at me for stealing her book when she found her copy in her desk drawer.

Chapter 3: ChadHurley.com

This is going to be the hard part. I only talked to Chad Hurley for a little over 2 hours in 1999, almost 15 years ago, but when I found out in 2011 Chad Hurley used the idea I gave him in 1999 to start YouTube in 2005, I did a lot of research on him. I have become a bit of an expert on Chad Hurley, but you could just as easily google Chad Hurley and read the same things I have for 3 years, but that would defeat the purpose of reading this chapter and, as the writer of this book, it would not allow you to understand my unique perspective on his character, so please read this chapter.

First, let's get the basics of Chad Hurley. To avoid the dreaded writer's block, I am going to copy and paste this from wikipedia...is that legal?...Who cares. Nobody is reading this yet...right?

Chad Meredith Hurley was born on January 24, 1977 in Reading, Pennsylvania. He was raised in a suburb or Reading called Birdsboro, PA. Chad got his bachelor's degree in graphic design from Indiana University of Pennsylvania. He is credited as the cofounder of YouTube.com with Steve Chen and Jawed Karim. Chad has had a string of failures since YouTube. He is considered a one hit wonder of the tech community. Despite his many failures, his net worth is somewhere around $350 million. Chad is the wealthiest person to ever graduate from our university, Indiana University of Pennsylvania.

Chad tried to start a formula one race team in the US as I suggested. Chad started a failed clothing store called Hlaska. Chad bought and crashed delicions.com. Delicious was popular and successful until Chad got ahold of it. Chad started a failing YouTube knockoff site called MixBit. He is currently being sued by Kim Kardashian and Kanye West for signing a contract stating he would not film their proposal and put it on the internet and then filming the proposal and putting it on the internet. In June 2006, he was voted 28th on Business 2.0's "50 People Who Matter Now" list. This and all the acclaim Chad has gotten are completely undeserved. In October 2006, he and Steve Chen sold YouTube for $1.65 billion to Google.Hurley worked in eBay's PayPal division. One of his tasks involved designing the original PayPal logo. I don't think he did anything but the logo for PayPal and have you ever taken a look at the PayPal logo? It is the most boring, simple logo on the internet. Before starting YouTube with fellow PayPal colleagues Steve Chen and Jawed Karim. Hurley was primarily responsible for the tagging and video sharing aspects of YouTube. I don't see how he contributed to this because he has no real programming abilities, but I did emphasise to Chad how important that aspect of the YouTube idea was, so I can see how he would want to concentrate on it. I don't think Chad really did anything meaningful for YouTube except the boring simple logo. I even told him I imagined the logo with the word You and a tv tube shape around the word "Tube", which is what the logo is.

Chad is the third child of Don and Joann Hurley, and grew up near Birdsboro, Pennsylvania. He has two siblings, an older sister, Heather, and a younger brother, Brent. Since childhood, Chad showed extreme interest in the arts, but then later became interested in computers and electronic media during high school. I spoke to Chad's mom, Joann. She was really nice until I mentioned the one percent promise Chad made to me, but took down my name and phone number and said she would pass it on to Chad.

He was a stand-out runner for Twin Valley High School's cross-country program, which won two of its PIAA State titles with him as a member in 1992 and 1994. He was also member of the Technology Student Association during high school. He graduated from Twin Valley High School (Pennsylvania), Elverson in 1995 and went on to receive his B.A. in Fine Art from Indiana University of Pennsylvania in 1999.

On October 16, 2006, Chen and Hurley sold YouTube to Google, Inc. for $1.65 billion. It was reported in the Wall Street Journal that Chad Hurley's share was $345.6M at Google's February 7, 2007 closing stock price of $470.01. He received 694,087 Google shares directly and another 41,232 shares in a trust. YouTube's other two co-founders, Steve Chen and Jawed Karim, received 625,366 shares and 137,443 shares, respectively valued at $326.2M and $64.6M. The Journal's report was based on Google's registration statement with SEC filed on February 7, 2007. Hurley stepped down as CEO of YouTube in October 2010 and stated he would stay on as an advisor of YouTube, allowing Salar Kamangar to take over the CEO position.

In August 2013, Chen and Hurley launched another company called MixBit which does video editing using smart phones. Steve Chen left MixBit shortly after hearing of the REAL YouTube story.

Chad was involved as a major investor with US F1 Team, one of the new entrants in Formula One automobile racing for the 2010 season. On March 2, 2010, the team's personnel were dismissed from their duties and the team was unofficially shut down. Neither Hurley, team principal Ken Anderson, or sporting director Peter Windsor would comment on the team's failure to make it to the grid. It is rumored that Hurley is still trying to get involved with F1 via other teams. Chad was quoted as saying "Next time, I will have Ferrari build me the car". I think he missed the point. I told him to start an American formula one team. That means American sponsors. You mean to tell me Ford, Chevy and none of the other American auto manufacturers would build a car for Chad? Ford made the "GT", a production vehicle that looks like a formula one car off the line.

Chad is, in general, a boring guy. And he is understandably private since he has alot to hide, like this book, TheREALYouTubeStory.com and the reality of his deceptions.. I apologize for the brevity of my explanation of Chad and his life, but just keep in mind that he is a lying, cheating, deceptive, stupid guy that was hell bent on success at any cost and I think we can move on.

Chapter 4: EricSkaggs.com vs ChadHurley.com

Eric Skaggs registered his first domain name in 1996. The first domain name Eric Skaggs registered was GoGetItNow.com , an internet portal that got as many as 10 million page views a day and generated as much as $5000 per month in revenue. Chad Hurley registered his first domain name in 2001. The first domain name Chad Hurley registered was ChadHurley.com, a simple personal page. Chad Hurley registered his second domain name in 2004. That domain name was YouTube.com, the domain name Eric Skaggs told him to register in 1999 5 years earlier.

Eric Skaggs was a Business major in college with an emphasis in computer science and finance. Chad Hurley was an art major in college and ran track. I challenge you to find me a major and sport that requires less academic abilities. Have you ever heard anybody say "I'm not smart enough to be an art major in college" or "I never learned how to run"?

To be more specific, Chad Hurley was a graphic design major. What is a graphic design major? A graphic design major is an art major with no artistic abilities. They used rulers and stencils because they couldn't make straight lines and accurate shapes and these days, they use programs like photoshop to make what they call art. The earliest remnant I can find of Chad Hurley's graphic designs is a stick figure of a man running that looks just like the guy on the walk signs. I think they still use this stick figure as the official logo of the IUP track and cross country teams. Is that art? I think not. Unless your definition of art is so broad that you believe a stick figure that mimicks a street sign is art.

I know you think I'm picking on Chad, but it emphasizes an important point. Chad knew his limitations. What's more important? Being smart or being a hard worker? A hard worker might spend his whole life in a mine where they would "go pound salt" as my grandmother often said to me when she wanted me to go away, but if you take that same hard worker, point him in the right direction, motivate and inspire him, and give him step by step instructions to follow like I did with Chad Hurley, that dumb hard worker can accomplish almost anything. A smart man without a good work ethic may never accomplish anything. The world is filled with poor geniuses. It is so common for a genius to be poor that it has become a cliche movie topic like Goodwill Hunting.

On the subject of morality, honesty and loyalty, Eric Skaggs served honorably in the Persian Gulf War and is a decorated war hero that was given top secret clearance after an extensive background check to determine his morality, honesty and loyalty. This is an honor that is bestowed upon very few of the most moral, honest and loyal people. Chad Hurley is being sued by Kim Kardashian and Kanye West for lying under signed contract, and although he admits he did lie, he is using his lawyers to not only try to get out of trouble, but to countersue those he hurt with his lies. Steve Chen and Jawed Karim also publically stated that Chad Hurley is a liar, specifically in regards to Chad's lie that he came up with the idea for YouTube.com. Chad did not come up with YouTube.com. I did.

Chapter 5: TheYouTubeGuy.com - How ChadHurley.com did what EricSkaggs.com told him to do

This is going to be a bit difficult because after I told Chad Hurley what to do to get my YouTube.com idea to work in 1999 during that fateful 2 hour conversation, I didn't even find out his last name until 2011 when I finally googled "chad iup youtube" and saw his picture. I thought the YouTube.com website was a big coincidence. How could I ever have imagined the millionaire founder of YouTube was the same dumb art major kid on a track scholarship at IUP, a crappy university, was the same guy that promised me 1% in exchange for the idea over 10 years ago. As I did my research, I found out Chad Hurley did exactly what I told him to do. He didn't deviate from what I told him to do for the next 12 years until I finally got a letter from his attorneys essentially telling me he would not give me the 1% he promised me for the YouTube.com idea I gave him. If he was smart, he would've fulfilled the promise he made to me in exchange for an ironclad nondisclosure agreement. I would've helped him hide the origins of the YouTube idea, my idea, to protect his stellar reputation and we could've worked together on MixBit.com and BuckGet.com. Instead, here I am telling all his dirty secrets. The three big secrets have the potential to destroy him and his reputation. His lawyers pointed these three big secrets out quite nicely. The first big secret is the "plausible story". That is the story I told Chad to tell people about how he came up with the idea. I told him to tell everyone he and some friends were at a party taking videos with camcorders and, if the technology was available, cell phones, and they couldn't share the videos with eachother so they created a website called YouTube.com to share their videos with eachother. Steve Chen and Jawed Karim both said Chad was lying about this, but when I told his lawyers what really happened, they attacked me. I wasn't the only one to say Chad was lying. The two men that have the most to lose from the lie also said Chad was lying. The second deception is the plan to meet and partner up with his cofounders, Steve Chen and Jawed Karim, at the internet company he could get a job at that ended up being PayPal.com. This destroys the relationship he has with Steve Chen, Jawed Karim and his friends and coworkers that were part of the plan at PayPal. The third secret would destroy his family. The secret that him marrying and getting Kathy Clark pregnant not necessarily in that order. Now his marriage to his wife and the conception of his children look like nothing but a part of the plan I laid out for Chad. If and when Kathy and her billionaire father, Jim Clark, find out they were nothing more than part of the plan I laid out for Chad Hurley in 1999 outside the Eberly College of Business computer lab at Indiana University of Pennsylvania, his reputation will be permanently destroyed.

When Chad and I parted ways outside Eberly College of Business at Indiana University of Pennsylvania, Chad jumped in his borrowed yellow Jeep Cherokee and went straight to the local grocery store, Giant Eagle. He bought the Wired Magazine and the Forbes List of the Richest People magazine, went to the track house, gathered the last of his things from the track/cross country house and headed back to Birdsboro, Pennsylvania. When he got to his parents house, he did what I told him to do and made two lists, a list of the internet companies he would redesign the logos for and a list of the richest internet billionaires. He went to his computer and started working on logos and sent them out to all the companies. He got a response from PayPal who offered him a job at PayPal. He accepted the job as a graphic designer for PayPal and headed to PayPal headquarters in California. When he got there, he befriended the smartest guys in the room, Steve Chen and Jawed Karim. He also found out Jim Clark, the billionaire founder of Silicon Graphics had a single daughter named Kathy Clark. He found out she was going to a birthday party so he decided to crash it. He didn't know anyone at the party but he was determined to meet Kathy. He went to the party and started buying Kathy Clark drinks. He drove her home, yadda yadda, and 9 months later they had their first child. When Kathy found out she was pregnant, Chad and Kathy got married. PayPal got bought by eBay and

Chad got a nice amount of cash from his stock options and used it and his connections through his billionaire heiress wife's father, Jim Clark, to find venture capital at Sequoia Capital. The domain name YouTube.com was registered by Chad Hurley in 2004. The site went live on valentines day 2005. YouTube.com grew quickly. I knew about YouTube.com but thought it was a big coincidence. Chad, Steve, and to a lesser degree Jawed, sold YouTube.com to , as I called it, a "company with more money than brains" (google) at the end of 2006 and the paperwork was filed at the beginning of 2007. YouTube was sold for $1.65 billion to google. The only really big stipulation is that Chad Hurley had to stay on as the CEO of YouTube.com, a division of Google.com, for 3 or 4 years. Google wanted Chad to stay on as CEO because he was the "brilliant" inventor of YouTube.com. They had no idea Chad was lying to them to get an inflated price for YouTube.com and Chad was paid $400,000 a year to be CEO of YouTube.com for a few years. Chad lied to Google to get a CEO position and probably an extra billion dollars for YouTube.com. I suggested to Chad's attorneys that Google got screwed too and maybe google should be on the same side as me, but his attorneys said Chad and Google were so in bed with one another that Google would never be on anyone's side but his.

Chapter 6: WhoInventedYouTube.com - When EricSkaggs.com found out about ChadHurley.com starting YouTube.com

This answers one of the most asked questions about this true story. Without understanding the answer to this question, many people have dismissed the truth. How did I not find out the guy I knew as Chad at IUP in 1999 outside Eberly College of Business computer lab was the guy that started YouTube.com in 2005 and sold it in 2007 and I didn't find out until 2011? I thought there was no way that dumb art major on a track scholarship from crappy IUP could've started YouTube. It must be a coincidence. He could've called it anything other than YouTube and I may have never figured it out. If Coryn Neff didn't tell me she thought the guy that started YouTube went to IUP, I may have never found out. If I hadn't done that search for "Chad IUP YouTube" and his picture came up and he looked just like he did in college...long hair, relatively tall and decent looking, I may have never found out. Sometimes I wonder what would've happened if I had looked into whether or not the guy that started YouTube was named Chad and went to IUP on a track scholarship and got a graphic design degree as soon as I found out about YouTube instead of thinking "that's a weird coincidence" if I might have been able to get ahold of Chad while he was still working on YouTube. Maybe he would've asked me to help with YouTube and maybe I would've went out to silicon valley and worked for YouTube right from the start. That sure would've made things easier and it would've made alot more sense for everyone instead of Chad needing to lie for the rest of his life to everyone. And I would much rather think of Chad as a good and honorable man than a liar, cheater and thief.

So, in 2011, I was living on the South Side of Pittsburgh about a block and a half from the hundreds of bars and clubs on carson street with my ex girlfriend Coryn Neff. She said something about YouTube and I told her the story about how I came up with the idea for YouTube and gave the whole idea to some guy named Chad outside Eberly College of Business computer lab in exchange for a verbal promise of 1%. I said "What a coincidence. And now this YouTube thing is huge". She said "Eric. You know the guy that started YouTube went to IUP don't you?" I said"No. I didn't know that. Wouldn't it be wild if his name is Chad?" So I went over to her laptop and googled "Chad IUP YouTube" and there he was. Chad Hurley. As i read through the articles, I realized he did everything I told him to do. Every last detail. Except for the 1% promise. "Maybe he's looking for me to fulfill his promise and to thank me for such a great idea". I tried to contact him on facebook, twitter linkedin, his email address, and any way I could find, but I couldn't get a response. I even got blocked from twitter. And then later, I got blocked from Facebook. Maybe he wasn't in control of his own social media. Alot of rich and famous people have other people control their social media.

I went back to my workaday life as a social worker, but couldn't let it go. I wrote a blog about the story and put it under the domain name IInventedYouTube.com. I later registered WhoInventedYouTube.com, TheYouTubeGuy.com, YouScrewd.com, TheRealYouTubeStory.com, TheYouTubeStory.com and RealYouTubeStory.com. I also recorded a little crappy one minute video and put it up on YouTube.com.

I found a guy named Herb Gilliland that not only said he invented YouTube, he actually filed a lawsuit and got five law firms/lawyers to represent him. I still don't understand his story. It doesn't make sense. He says he called PayPal in

2004 and talked to either Chad Hurley or Steve Chen. How could you not tell the difference? And neither of them worked there in 2004. They both left in 2003. His video says something like he programmed Chad Hurley's brain waves with the YouTube idea. What does that even mean? His story about how he came up with the YouTube name makes even less sense. And why would you call customer service at PayPal and get the graphic designer that doesn't even work there? Did he have a customer service issue with the logo? None of his story makes any sense because it is all a huge and not even good lie but he got five law firms to represent him and I had to struggle to get one lawyer to send one letter for me and my story makes sense and is true. That seems really strange to me, but I, to this day, have never sued anyone or had any legal issues. I don't even really have a lawyer.

I kept thinking "Chad owes me $16.5 million and he may be trying to find me". So I started looking for lawyers that might be able to help me. I must've contacted hundreds of attorneys before I found one that would help me. His name was Louis Kroeck. He was a young, aggressive attorney but a really nice, fun loving guy. He even had a really popular facebook group called Pittsburgh Happy Hour that went out to happy hours in Pittsburgh, obviously. He read the story at IInventedYouTube.com and was intrigued. I explained to Lou that I just wanted an answer as to whether or not Chad was looking for me to fulfill the $16.5 million promise. I realized that alot of time had passed and that the statute of limitations may have already passed but that maybe he was looking for me to give me the $16.5 million he promised me. He was intrigued and wrote a letter for me and sent it to his address certified mail so we could be sure he got it.

Chad did get Lou's letter, and about two weeks later, we got a letter back from his attorneys, Wilson, Sonsini, Goodrich and Rosati. They are Google's attorneys. They are huge and powerful. And all the letter did was reiterate the main points of contention of the story verbatim and then threaten me and Lou. Lou was done and I was done from a legal perspective. Now, it was time to go at this from a moral perspective. You know what they say. Exhaust all options of diplomacy and then go to war. There was no way to resolve this legally. But I still had what I like to call the three t's...Time, Truth and The first amendment.

So I started writing this book. I never realized what a pain in the ass writing a book is. And I type a fairly respectable 50 words a minute. But this is something I am truly passionate about and I think alot of people can learn alot of valuable lessons from this so I will keep on pecking at this damn keyboard until it is finished.

My hope is that this book will be well received by people, that many people will enjoy it and learn from it, and that Chad will be revealed as the fraud I know him to be and I will get the acclaim I deserve. It would be nice if this book was the answer to making things right about this situation. I still feel there must be a way to resolve this, but until then, this book is all I have...this and my new startup, BuckGet.com.

Chapter 7: BuckGet.com - EricSkaggs.com starts his own website and ChadHurley.com starts MixBit.com

When I started telling people that I Invented YouTube, I got exacly what I expected...a great deal of eye rolling skepticism. And I understand that. After all, most people didn't know that I had a brief brush with .com success with GoGetItNow.com in the late 90's amd early 2000's. And even if they did, they would ask "If you came up with the whole idea for YouTube from domain name to exit strategy and everything in between, why didn't you do it yourself?" I will be the first to admit that is a good question, but YouTube was not the type of website I wanted to create. I wanted to create a website where people could achieve their dreams with from a financial and entrepreneurial perspective. GoGetItNow.com was a combination of the search capabilities of Yahoo, the free email of hotmail and the free web pages of geocities, but at it's core, I wanted to be able to help people earn a living online. After all, my background was in finance, not art. And GoGetItNow.com was making $5000 a month and doubling every couple of months and got as many as 10 million page views a day 5 years before Chad registered the YouTube.com domain name I told him to register. Enough people suggested that I should start over where I left off when the GoGetItNow.com domain name was taken from me by the call center worker at Network Solutions that I finally decided to start over. The first thing I did was try to register a bunch of domain names that were getting traffic but that no one owned so I could send the wayward traffic to affiliate programs and make more money than I was making with my day job as a social worker. I used a misspell generator to generate all of the common misspellings of Match.com and registered 9 domain names. I don't remember them all but some of them were mahtch.com mawtch.com and stuff like that. I used promo codes and got the domain names for 99 cents each so it only cost me about $10. I redirected the domain names to the Match.com affiliate program. The first month, I made $100...not bad. The second month I made $200 and realized it was going to double every month, but for how many months? I found out the Match.com affiliate cookies stayed active in visitors browsers for 6 months. That meant in the third month, I was going to make $400 and I did. In the fourth month, I was going to make $800, fifth $1600 and sixth $3200! That was more than I was making as a caseworker for the government! I was hooked! If I registered 400 domain names and did the same thing, I would make 40 times $3200 or $128,000 a month! I started registering a ton of domain names. I had over 400 domain names and was doing really well until I realized that internet companies don't like that way of sending traffic to their sites. The company that was sending me my affiliate checks, commission junction, sent me my last $1000 check and shut me down. I tried to reason with them but they said it violated their terms of service agreement and I wasn't going to get paid anymore. I just spent something like $1000 on domain names to make $2000. Some people would call that a fairly successful first attempt. I almost made more than I was at my decent $40,000 a year government social work job. That was my goal. When I made more on the internet than I did at my full time government job, I would quit and dedicate myself to internet business full time. I came close, and I was considering quitting just because now I saw that it was possible. I decided to call my first internet business in over 10 years TheGreatestSites.com. I wasn't in love with the domain name, but it captured what I hoped to have someday...the greatest sites. My employer kind of made the decision for me though when they extended my probation period from 6 months to 8 months. It was extremely stressful. They gave me almost four times as many cases to be evaluated. I was singled out from the 20 or so coworkers. It was strange because I had the highest civil service test score in the state. With my veteran's preference and excellent test taking abilities, I got 104%. Naturally, I got a 94%, but because I was a veteran, they gave me an extra 10%. I remember the girl that went to Carnegie Mellon, a very prestigious university, that bragged about how she was a genius. She got the same natural test score I got. That makes sense. I have an IQ of somewhere between 138 and 148 depending on whether or not you use the actual IQ test or the ones you can take online. I prefer to use the 148 from the IQ test online. Either one of the scores makes my IQ higher than Einstein's, although there are different IQ test scales and I have heard lots of different things about Einstein's IQ. Anyways, I like to say I have a higher IQ than Einstein and I was 16 my senior year of high school even though it was only for 2 weeks...it is still true right?

So they laid me off from that crappy social work job and I was happy they did. I wanted to quit anyways. They laid off the only three white male veterans. I filed a claim with the state, but I knew it wouldn't go anywhere. What was the state going to do? Sue themselves for unfair layoffs? I was able to collect unemployment compensation, proof that it was a layoff. Even though it was clearly extremely unfair, I accepted it because I hated the job and wanted to work on internet businesses. I finally figured out what I needed to do. I transitioned from domaining to developing. Now, I needed a brand. I wanted it to be about my background, finance. So I went to an online thesaurus and looked up all of the synonyms for money. There were something like 30. I put them through a bulk domain name submitter with .com on the end of them. They were all taken. So I looked up all the synonyms for make. There were about 30 of those. I used a permutation generator to come up with all the possible combinations of the words make and money. There were about 10 million. Then, I put those 10 million phrases into a bulk domain submitter. 9 million were taken. I took the 1 million that were available and put them through google webmaster tools 2000 at a time and laid them out on an excel spreadsheet to see which domain names were searched for the most. Of all the domain names, BuckGet was searched for the most on google. It was searched for 73 times globally that month. It was also the shortest domain name that contained synonyms of the words make and money. It also had the same amount of letters and YouTube and contained the word get just like my first domain name from the 90's, GoGetItNow.com. There were so many special things about the domain name BuckGet.com that it seemed like fate. Some people tell me they don't like the domain name. I challenge them to come up with a better one. One guy that said he doesn't like it runs a website called BudgetSimple.com. How many websites that are very popular have 12 letters and 4 syllables? Google...2 syllables 6 letters. Facebook...2 syllables 8 letters. YouTube 2 syllables 7 letters. Twitter...2 syllables 7 letters. The only notable exception is Wikipedia.org, but that is a crazy outlyer in this statistical analysis. BuckGet...2 syllables 7 letters. And just 6 months after I made the site live, BuckGet.com was more popular than BudgetSimple.com had been after being around for 10 years so fuck you. Fuck all of you. BuckGet.com is an awesome domain name. And it only cost me 99 cents. Around the same time I started

BuckGet.com, Chad Hurley and Steve Chen bought MixBit.com and MixBits.com for about $3000 each. So they were already spending 6000 times more than I was. And that's appropriate because Chad had 6000 times more money than I had and so did Steve. Steve left MixBit though so it is truly me vs Chad in this comparison. I think Steve found out he was the asian guy in the plan I gave Chad and left him because the day I tweeted BuckGet.com was doing better than MixBit.com, Steve Chen left MixBit and went to work at Google Ventures. It may have been a coincidence, but it's still kind of funny right? I bet Chad's wife will leave him when I get this published. And I bet her father will hire lawyers to crush Chad. That would be fair. Wouldn't it be funny if Chad ends up broke and I end up being rich and successful? They say kharma is a bitch. But let's help it out by actually doing something. Right? So I started BuckGet.com with $60,000 and Chad started MixBit with $360,000,000 , exactly 6000 times what I have. He also hired 100 people and I am on my own. And his bandwidth probably costs $18,000 a month while mine is about $3 a month...exactly 6000 times less. So what does it mean if BuckGet.com gets more traffic than MixBit.com? Does that mean I am better than Chad Hurley at website development? No. It means I am 6000 times better than Chad Hurley at website development. So if Chad was able to get $350 million from the YouTube idea I gave him, I should be able to get 6000 times $350 million or $210 trillion from BuckGet.com? Sounds crazy right? Wait till you hear the idea. It is also worth noting, and maybe I should've mentioned this before, that Chad Hurley has never made a penny on the internet. As a matter of a fact, since he gave up 80 percent of YouTube.com just to keep it going, he actually spent 80 percent of $1.65 billion just to get it going and keep it going until he sold it. BuckGet.com was profitable almost immediately upon its launch. I wonder how long it took google to realize they just bought an idea from and hired a moron. But I digress. So here's what BuckGet.com is all about.

Everyone talks about disrupting trillion dollar industries. Changing the way people in that industry do things. Doing them better, faster, smarter. What about disrupting the entire employment industry? How much is the employment industry worth? It must be worth...thousands of trillions whatever that is. Quadrillions? That's what BuckGet.com will do.

Did you ever look for a job and find yourself applying to endless jobs that you don't even like but you need a job? They say you should treat getting a job like it is a job. Well what if instead of sitting down at your computer and looking for your dream job for weeks, months and sometimes years, you used that time, effort and energy to actually create your dream job and just start doing it right at your computer or smartphone? That would be awesome right? Well it is here...it is called BuckGet.com.

The first thing I tried to do with BuckGet.com was to try to make a better google.com. How do you convince people to use a search engine that isn't google? Pay them. BuckGet.com started out as a search engine that pays you. That didn't even go live because I crashed Commission Junction's servers. The next obvious target was number two in the world, Facebook. I launched BuckGet.com on March 30, 2013 as FacebookForEntrepreneurs.com. It was the world's first and only truly useful and totally free social network dedicated to helping people find a way to earn a living online. It was extremely successful...almost too successful. At about the one year mark, BuckGet.com had over 700,000 members. It was growing virally and got about 100,000 page views per day. The only problem was it was ad supported and the ads were only generating about $30 in revenue per month. That was enough to stay profitable since the site only cost $3 a month to run, but this wasn't sustainable. And the servers were starting to throw up server busy errors. If I upgraded the servers, it would no longer be profitable. And even though the ads were for ebooks about how to make money online, people constantly signed up and messaged me "How do I make money at BuckGet.com?" I was just telling them to order the ebooks in the ads around the site, but they weren't ordering very many. So I did some research and found out there was a nice way to make money online called microjobbing. I guess fiverr.com started this. So I found a script that mimicked fiverr and pivoted into a microjob site. The general idea of BuckGet.com at that point was what can you do for people and how much will you charge them? A good example is "I will MAKE YOU A WEBSITE for $500". Get it? Good. It worked out really well, but I couldn't invite the original 717,162 members from the social network version of BuckGet.com so it was like starting over with a 717,162 member mailing list. Not a bad restart and at least it answered the question as to how people could make money at BuckGet.com. So I started making a few hundred dollars a month, and a few people were making a dollar here and there, but it still wasn't where I wanted it to be. I am still working on it, but it is headed in the right direction. In the future, I see BuckGet.com as a repository of all ways to earn a living online. When I ask you where I should go to search for something, you think "google" . When I ask you where you can buy something online, you think "amazon". What do you think of when I say "earn a living online"? Someday soon, I hope it will be BuckGet.com. In the meantime MixBit.com sucks. And Chad Hurley is getting sued by Kim Kardashian and Kanye West for crashing their engagement party at ATandT stadium in San Francisco, signing a legal document saying he would not film the proposal and put it on the internet, walking in and filming it and putting it on the internet at MixBit.com to try to get the website some publicity. MixBit got a little bit of publicity, but it still sucks.

Chapter 8: TheREALYouTubeStory.com - Reaction from ChadHurley.com , his attorneys, friends, family, coworkers and the tech community.

The three reactions I get when I tell people I am TheYouTubeGuy.com and IInventedYouTube.com are the "eye rolling skeptic" or what I like to call the "closed minded assholes", the "genuinely interested" or what I like to call the "wide eyed open minded understanding people", and the "I am sick of hearing this story" crowd or what I like to call "friends and family". Chad himself is, I guess, in a fourth category. Chad is in the category of what I like to call "a lying, cheating, thieving dishonest asshole".

The first person that ever knew TheRealYouTubeStory.com was Coryn Neff, my ex girlfriend. She was there when I first had the stark revelation that the founder of YouTube went to IUP and googled "Chad IUP YouTube" and found out it was Chad Hurley, the guy I gave the YouTube idea to in 1999 that promised me one percent of the company that he ended up selling for $1.65 billion. Coryn was genuinely interested in the YouTube story but suggested I get back into internet business instead of encouraging me to ask Chad if he would give me what he promised me that amounted to $16.5 million for the YouTube idea I gave him. I did what she suggested and didn't really reach out to Chad. I was pretty busy trying to get through the probationary period at my social work job.

The second person I ever told about how I gave Chad Hurley the idea for YouTube from domain name to exit strategy was, I believe, Jim Jen. I may have mentioned it to my family and friends, but I hadn't really done the research to really tell the story very well, so I don't really recall their reaction and I think it was fairly negative and dismissed. I don't think my family and friends thought I was lying. I just don't remember getting any strong opinions from them. Jim Jen is the guy in charge of an internet business incubator in Pittsburgh called Alphalab. I think I first found out about Alphalab from googleing something like "Pittsburgh internet business" or something like that. I found out Alphalab would give you $25,000 for 5% of your internet business which would make it worth $500,000. So I applied to Alphalab with something like seven different ideas I had. Jim and I had an interview at Alphalab where he gave me some advice about focusing on one idea instead of scattering my efforts around seven ideas. He also suggested I may have a better chance if I worked on my internet business idea full time instead of being distracted by my full time social work job. This prompted me to consider leaving my job, but I didn't yet because I hadn't settled on one great idea yet. Jim asked me if I had any previous experience with internet business and I told him about my website in the 90's, GoGetItNow, and how it was doing great. I said it got as many as 10 million page views a day, generated as much as $5000 a month and was doubling every other month or so but that the domain name was taken by a call center worker in India that worked for Network Solutions. Jim asked me if I had any other successes in internet business, and I shyly mentioned that I gave Chad Hurley the idea for YouTube when we went to IUP together. I hadn't really had a chance to do the research to figure out how to tell the story just yet. I guess he looked into it, because when I got the denial email from Alphalab, I called him and had a conversation with him about, once again, focusing my efforts on one great idea, getting rid of distractions like my full time job, and Jim mentioned that he or someone had looked into my YouTube story and the only thing that was verifiable was that we both went to IUP at the same time. I guess that was something, but I think it was seen as more of a negative than a positive. Jim suggested that I get in touch with Chad. He was the only person that knew my ideas were good and worked because the idea I gave him worked. And he promised me 1% of what amounted to $16.5 million. Maybe Chad would want to work with me on some other world changing ideas. I have alot more ideas.

Then I started telling everyone about the YouTube story. I realized that Chad and I had two mutual friends on facebook. One was my old roommate, Mike Dixon. Mike was a computer science major at IUP. I called him and asked him how he knew Chad. He said when he was in ROTC, the ROTC people and the track team used to run around the IUP track together every morning. When Chad found out Mike was a computer science major, Chad started running around the track with Mike picking his brains about computer stuff. I asked Mike if he had ever given Chad any good ideas like I did with the YouTube idea. Mike said no. We talked a bit about the YouTube story and Mike told me the story made sense to him because he knew I was working on some things on the internet years before Chad was anything more than an art major on a track scholarship at IUP. That was my first real positive response to the YouTube story with some validation from someone that knew me at IUP.

After a while, it seemed like everyone I knew was at least in some way familiar with the YouTube story. I was sharing the story with everyone all over the internet and in the real world. My friend Shawn Delaney from Indiana Pennsylvania called me one day and said "Guess who was in Indiana today?"

I said"No way. Chad Hurley came back to IUP? Why?"

Shawn said his dad was at the grand opening of the new Kovalchick center, a large basketball arena, at IUP. Apparently, Chad donated a million dollars to IUP to get the Kovalchick center dedicated to his track coach. At the grand opening of the center, Chad was sitting in the first row with the other contributors. Apparently, Chad sat right next to my friend Shawn's dad.

Shawn told me his dad asked Chad "What is a young guy like you doing sitting in the front row with the contributors?"

Chad said"I'm the YouTube guy".

Shawn's dad said"What's YouTube?"

Chad said "It is a website. Ask your kids".

So when Shawn's dad came home he asked Shawn what YouTube was. Shawn asked why and his dad said he sat next to the guy that started some company called YouTube at the grand opening of the Kovalchick center. Shawn called me to tell me. Unfortunately, the event took place a few days before Shawn called me and Chad had already left IUP. Otherwise, I would have gone to IUP to pay a visit to Chad. That would have been fun.

I guess the million dollar donation Chad made to IUP played a pretty big part in the IUP Alumni Association wanting to separate themselves from me. When I went to Alumni functions, the president of the Alumni Association would tell me they didn't want to get involved. I understand that. That's why I don't want to get any more calls from the Alumni Association asking for money. When they call me, I tell them I will also give them a million dollars like Chad did if they help me resolve the YouTube situation. The people that call me from the alumni association are usually very understanding and sometimes I think they take my offer seriously. They should. I would give them a million dollars if they come up with some way to help me get the $16.5 million Chad promised me for the YouTube idea. I would give anyone the one million dollars if they helped me. And if IUP accepted the fact that the YouTube idea was conceived of at IUP instead of at Menlo Park, California, the lie Chad tells the world, it may help the university more than they can possibly imagine.

So I tried to get in touch with Chad through Facebook, Twitter, and all the social networks he was on that I found at ChadHurley.com . Chad didn't respond, but I figured alot of rich and famous people don't control their own social media. I couldn't assume Chad was maliciously ignoring me. I even tried to connect to Chad's connections. Some of them followed me back. The only people that blocked me were Chad and his brother. Maybe they block alot of people. I got a really great private investigator to help me find Chad's contact information. He asked me not to name names, but he was willing to help me for free because I guess he was intrigued by the story and he is a friend of the family. I tried to call all the phone numbers and one of them out of the ten worked. I talked to Chad Hurley's housekeeper. I think her name was Anne. She was very nice. I told her how I gave Chad the whole idea for YouTube from domain name to exit strategy. I didn't tell her about the 1% he promised me because I thought that was unnecessary and I didn't want her to think I was just after money. It wasn't just about money. I told her I had some new ideas, which I did, and I was hoping Chad would want to work on them with me. She said she was sure he would want to talk to me and work with me. She took down my name and phone number and said she would give him the message. She asked me how I got the phone number. I did look the number up on the internet and found it listed as Kathy Clark's phone number. I told her I found it on the internet. I never got a call back from Chad and when I tried to call the number again a few weeks later, the number had been disconnected and no further information was available. I used the email addresses that I was given by my awesome private investigator to email him a very nice friendly email asking him to get in touch with him. I got no response. I emailed one of the early investors in YouTube, Roelof Botha. I told him the whole story and he sent me an email back thanking me for the "color". I am pretty sure he was calling me a liar. He never contacted me again. I tried to get in touch with Steve Chen and Jawed Karim, but never got a response. At least they didn't block me, but they never followed or friended me back.

One day, I was watching a movie called Cottage Country with my girlfriend, Robin. In the movie, the guy accidentally killed his brother and then he and his fiancee ended up having to kill his brother's girlfriend and a few of his friends to cover it up. The killer guy was finally convinced to come clean when his mom cried and begged him to do the right thing. I said to Robin "Wouldn't it be funny if I called Chad Hurley's mom and asked her to convince Chad to do the right thing?" Robin was kind of against the idea, but I looked up Chad's parents phone number and gave her a call before I lost my nerve and chickened out. She was very nice while I told her the whole story. She got a bit less nice when I mentioned the one percent Chad promised me. She told me all she could do was take my name and phone number and ask Chad to call me. I never got a call back and I haven't had the nerve to call her again, although I might at some point. Maybe she will tell me that she talked to Chad and he told her the truth. That he did promise me 1% for the YouTube idea. Maybe Chad's mom will get him to do the right thing. Or maybe the number has been changed like Chad's.

At this point, I still didn't have any idea if Chad was ignoring me on purpose or if he was just really busy, but he definitely wasn't actively looking for me. I was running out of ideas for how to get an answer from Chad personally, so I started looking around for an attorney that would help me reach out to Chad. The first of hundreds of lawyers I tried to contact that wanted to meet with me was that crazy guy, Herbert Gilliland's attorney. Herb is that crazy guy that had that non story for how he thinks he gave Chad the idea for YouTube through brain waves over the telephone. Herb lives in Pittsburgh and I asked him to meet with me but he won't. I went to Herb's attorney dressed in my favorite suit and we went into a conference room where I told him the story and he said he couldn't do anything for me because it would be a conflict of interest. I thanked him for his time and told him"At least now you know the real story". He suggested I continue to reach out to Chad and any other attorneys that might be able to help.

The next attorney that was willing to talk to me seriously about helping resolve the situation was Lou Kroeck. He was a really cool guy. He struck me as a young, hungry lawyer that really wanted to help people. He was intrigued by the story and understanded that I just needed an answer from Chad, so he wrote a very nice letter to Chad asking for a conversation. We sent the letter by certified mail and about 12 days later, we got a very strongly worded letter from Chad's attorneys threatening both me and Lou. Sometime around then, I got a tweet from a guy named Troy Osinoff. He asked me if Chad and I had talked about the story. I said no but I was trying to get ahold of him. Chad chimed in with a bunch of negative tweets calling me a catfish or internet liar and Chad tweeted that he didn't know me and said he thought I was crazy and needed help. I didn't respond right away. I just took screenshots of the tweets and sent them to Lou. Lou said there wasn't much we could do about the negative tweets.

I realized that it was up to me to get the story to as many people as possible and thought it would be ironic if I would offer anyone that could help me get the 1 percent Chad owed me 1 percent of what I got or $165,000. I realized that wasn't a very impactful amount to promise anyone to help me so I upped the reward to $1 million. I got some responses and a few were helpful but they haven't resolved the situation yet. I am still hopeful that someone will come up with a great idea or that maybe Chad will come to his senses and I will wake up one morning and find a $16.5 million check in my mailbox. I would even sign a nondisclosure agreement and renounce the real YouTube story by saying this is a work of fiction. It would be a lie, but if Chad comes to his senses, it would be in both of our best interests to protect his reputation so that we could possibly work together on some new ideas. I am conflicted by that last sentence, and even as I typed it, I am not sure I can lie about something I feel so strongly about. What would you do? I guess most people would lie and say something like "My integrity is not for sale" or something like that, but $16.5 million is alot of money. I guess that is a decision I will have to make if and when the situation is presented to me.

I told everyone that would listen the real youtube story. I even got the custom license plate in Pennsylvania that says YOUTUBE and put WWW.THEYOUTUBEGUY.COM on my car around the YouTube plate. When BuckGet.com started doing very well, I replaced the YouTube plate with a custom plate that says BUCKGET and put WWW.BUCKGET.COM on the back of my car and I put the YOUTUBE plate on the front of my car.

The first person to tell me in the Pittsburgh technology community to be quiet about the YouTube story was an inner school teacher named Josh Lucas that fell ass backwards into the tech community of Pittsburgh by getting a friend that works for USA Today to write up a contract stating USA Today would give him $300,000 to make them a crowdfunding website called Crowdasaurus.com. USA Today backed out of the contract after Crowdasaurus was given $25,000 by Alphalab. Crowdasaurus shut down after never succeeding in one crowdfunding campaign. Josh took the $25,000 Alphalab gave him and rolled it over into a coworking workspace that rents desks for $150 a month called The Hardware Store. The Hardware Store is now competing with Alphalab and is welcoming internet business startups into their own internet business incubator. I have to hand it to Josh. He is having a go at it and he seems to have the passion and drive necessary to succeed. His real strenght, in my opinion, is his ability to convince people to listen to and believe in him. Unfortunately, I am not one of those people. When Josh told me people were talking about me and know who I am, I said"That sounds like a good thing. There is no such thing as bad publicity". Josh said "Yes there is". I disagree with him. Every time somebody tells me I need to shut up about the truth, it just makes me want to tell the YouTube story more.

There seems to be a bit of a negative whisper campaign against me in the Pittsburgh technology community, but that just strengthens my resolve. I want people to talk about it. I want everyone to talk about it. Opinions, whether they are negative or positive, are welcome. What is your opinion?

Chapter 9: What EricSkaggs.com is doing now - BuckGet.com , YouScrewd.com : TheREALYouTubeStory.com , $1 million reward, book, movie, etc.

So by now you know what I am doing now. I have a successful profitable startup called BuckGet.com and I am writing this book, YouScrewd.com : TheREALYouTubeStory.com .

Today is veterans day, 2014 and I just got an email from Alphalab, one of the big internet business incubators in Pittsburgh. It said they weren't interested in BuckGet.com. This was the third time I applied to Alphalab and the second time I applied with BuckGet.com. I was confused about their choice to send out denial emails on veteran's day. Especially since I am a veteran. And tomorrow, they are having their big biannual demo day where the previous businesses that were selected into Alphalab show what their companies do. There are going to be alot of pissed off people at demo day tomorrow that got denial letters the day before. They could've at least waited to send out denial letters until after demo day and veterans day.

The class of startups that got into Alphalab last cycle that will be presenting at demo day tomorrow are covey, sitwith, researchwe, datasquid, nebulus and easely. Not one of these companies has the .com associated with their brand. They are either obscure country codes that they could lose any time the countries decide to pull them off the internet or long tailed domain names with several confusing or made up words in them. Not one of them would fit on a license plate like BuckGet. Not one of them contains just words that are in the dictionary with a .com at the end. The only idea worth mentioning is easely.co. I like the idea of subscribing to a service that lets you swap out your art when you get tired of it. It is like netflix for art. It isn't something I would be interested in but I can see how some art snobs might be interested in it. But, as I said, they don't even own the .com domain name for their own non english dictionary words domain. That's three strikes against them on day one. A quick analysis of all the companies incubated by Alphalab in the past 6 months shows that almost all of them are extremely unpopular. The most popular website is easely.co. Over the past 6 months, easely's highest ranking in popularity was 1,910,852 in the world. In the past 6 months, BuckGet.com's highest ranking in popularity was 120,272 in the world. And all of the companies incubated by Alphalab started with at least $25,000 and were given a value of $500,000. BuckGet.com started with a dollar and was never given a value, although a quick valuation shows the value of BuckGet.com at about $22 million. What is Alphalab thinking? How are they evaluating companies that they accept into their incubator? Jim Jen was asked how they evaluate startups the last time I went to an event at Alphalab, and he really couldn't answer the question. He basically said Alphalab accepts companies they like. What does that mean? I think it means they don't know what they are doing.

There is still hope for BuckGet.com. There is another incubator in Pittsburgh called ThrillMill that seems interested in incubating BuckGet. I will find out soon, but I won't hold my breath. I don't think the Pittsburgh technology community is very supportive of me or BuckGet. I think it has something to do with the YouTube story, but I can't rule out the possibility that Pittsburgh is just a bad place to start an internet business. I often say sometimes I feel like I would be better off starting an internet business on a deserted island with a laptop and internet access than in the unsupportive, underfunded and Carnegie Mellon University obsessed Pittsburgh technology community. We will see just how right I am. I might end up moving to New York or Silicon Valley. New York makes sense. My brother and sister both work for Yahoo in New York. My brother is a computer programmer and my sister is in internet marketing. When BuckGet is as successful as I know it will be, I could appoint myself the Chief BuckGetter, my brother could be the Chief Technical BuckGetter, my sister could be the Chief Marketing BuckGetter and my sister's fiancee, a hedge fund manager in New York, could be the Chief Investment BuckGetter. That would be awesome and it makes alot of sense. I don't really know anybody in Silicon Valley. The only person I have ever met that is considered a successful internet businessperson in Silicon Valley is Chad Hurley, but it doesn't look like he wants to work with me. I still consider Silicon Valley to be my Mecca, and I often look for apartments in the Silicon Valley area, but it doesn't make much sense to move there unless I get some support from that area. If a venture capitalist or angel investor from Silicon Valley saw BuckGet on f6s.com or Angellist.com or somewhere in the internet and called me up and said"I like what you are doing with BuckGet.com and I like where you're going with it. I would love to invest a million dollars in BuckGet.com for ten percent of the company and mentor and support you and your startup, but you live in Pittsburgh and I am in Silicon Valley. Would you be able to move to Silicon Valley?" I am almost positive I would say yes.

BuckGet.com doesn't really need incubated. It only costs about a dollar a month to run and I make about $200 a month from it. I just know BuckGet.com is the next big thing, and I won't give up until BuckGet is a multi billion dollar corporation. I am giving myself the same ten years Chad Hurley had from the time I gave him the YouTube idea in 1999 to the time Chad fulfilled the contract with google in about 2010. Most people think YouTube started in 2005 and they sold it to google in 2007, but I know I gave Chad the idea in 1999 and he didn't fulfill his obligations to google until about 2010. So it really took Chad about 10 years, and I am giving myself the same 10 years. I don't have the benefit of a .com job like Chad, who squeaked into an art position at Paypal by following my advice, I don't live in Silicon Valley, and I didn't knock up the heiress to a multi billion dollar empire like I told Chad to do, but I have the brains. Chad didn't and doesn't have brains. The one person I have met in the Pittsburgh technology community that says he met Chad at an internet business conference in Seattle, Gene Evangelist, said Chad struck him as a "frat boy surfer type". I couldn't have put it better myself. That is exactly the impression I got from Chad. Especially when I asked him if he went to any of the bars and clubs in Indiana and he told me he and his buddies from the cross country house just had parties there. The cross country house was basically a frat house. And when Chad took his baseball cap off and exposed his long hair, I told him he already had that west coast surfer look. Now that you know Chad didn't come up with the YouTube idea like he says he did, tell me one thing Chad has done that indicates he is intelligent. At best, you can say Chad did exactly what he was told to do verbatim. I guess that could be considered a kind of intelligence. The ability to steal an idea, recognize it is a good idea, and do it exactly as you were told to do.

Now about this book, YouScrewd.com : TheREALYouTubeStory.com . I am really happy that I finally have an interesting and compelling true story to tell. I never really considered myself much of a writer, but I always dreamed of writing a book. I think most people do. I just never had a story to tell that I was passionate about to the extent that I could write a book about it. If you are reading this, you know where I am at in the writing of this book....I am riiiiiiiight....here! But what do I hope to do with this book? I guess I will self publish it. I tried contacting publishers and really got no responses. Then, I found out it is a good idea to get a literary agent. I emailed pretty much all of them, and only got one positive response. One literary agent said "If you have a klout.com score of above 50, I will be your literary agent". I responded back with a screenshot of my klout.com score showing that I have a klout score of 64. I assumed the literary agent would be interested, but I never got a response after that. I thought about calling them, but I have also heard that a literary agent doesn't really do anything significant but take 10 percent of all the author's hard work and put it in their pocket. They are basically, relatively unnecessary middlemen.

Chapter 10: The Future of BuckGet.com, YouScrewd.com, EricSkaggs.com and ChadHurley.com

So here's the future of BuckGet.com, YouScrewd.com, EricSkaggs.com and ChadHurley.com. I will self publish YouScrewd.com. It won't be that popular at first, but enough people will read the story and understand it that Chad will be permanently discredited in the internet business community. People that read the book will make efforts to get the $1 million I am offering to get the $16.5 million Chad promised me for the YouTube idea.

If Chad is smart, he will offer me $16.5 million as soon as possible to stop the truth, this book, from gaining too much momentum. If Chad gives me the $16.5 million he promised me, I and everyone else that finds out about this story or reads this book will leave him alone. I will help him with his new endeavors like mixbit. I know how to fix mixbit.

If Chad doesn't give me the $16.5 million, Chad's wife, Kathy Clark, will leave him and Chad will lose nearly everything. He will lose his money, his houses, his cars, his children and his wife. Also, his business relationships will be permanently damaged. Steve Chen, Roelof Botha, Jim Clark, Jawed Karim and everyone that helped Chad do what I told him to do will sue him and withdraw their support and he will lose the rest of what he worked for and never be able to get back on his feet. This book will be turned into a movie and everyone will find out the truth, that Chad Hurley is a fraud. He will lose all of his friends who now see him as a scam artist, liar and cheater that was using them the whole time. Even Chad's family will shun him as they realize he was lying to them the whole time.

YouScrewd will become a bestseller and the movie will be a blockbuster. I will more than make up for the $16.5 million Chad promised me for the YouTube idea.

As the book and movie get more and more popular and my credibility increases in the internet business community. Investors will recognize the potential of BuckGet.com and invest heavily in my business. I will use the investments to take BuckGet.com to the next level and change the way people work by allowing them to pursue their dream jobs right from their computers. The word "Buckget" will be added to the dictionary and will be defined as "earning a living online" the way "google" is in the dictionary as "search the internet".

BuckGet will generate enough revenue to be eligible for inclusion into NASDAQ as the ticker symbol BUCK and/ or NYSE as GET. The IPO will launch at around a dollar a share and will skyrocket as worldwide members realize the value of BuckGet.

Indiana University of Pennsylvania and the Alumni Association will finally accept the real YouTube story and Eric Skaggs will get the credit he deserves as the billionaire founder of BuckGet.com the inventor of YouTube and the bestselling author of YouScrewd. Chad will become penniless and homeless. He will spend the rest of his life trying to steal his next big idea to no avail as no one will want to work with him or share ideas with him. IUP will recognize Eric Skaggs as the wealthiest graduate of the university and Eric Skaggs will get IUP's president's award and Chad Hurley's awards for "innovation" will be retracted by IUP and all the other organizations that gave Chad undeserved acclaim.

Now it's time for the call to action. Go to ChadHurley.com, google "Chad Hurley", connect with him, send him emails, call him, his friends and family members and do what you can to make Chad do the right thing. Go to IInventedYouTube.com, TheYouTubeGuy.com and WhoInventedYouTube.com, contribute ideas, and if any of them work out, you will get $1 million. I am counting on you. I would love to give one or several of you $1 miillion. So let's do it. Let's do the right thing and hold Chad accountable for his lies.

My greatest hope, other than resolving this situation amicably, is that you, the reader, will develop a better understanding of how YouTube really came to be and derive the lessons within to better yourself and those around you to become a better and more ethical person. To learn what it takes to succeed and to maintain success. To be the person you know you can be and to be open and honest during your journey to success. And I wouldn't mind giving you a million dollars.